The Art of Bonsai

A Beginner's Guide to Cultivating, Shaping, and Creating Living Masterpieces

Kyo Itakura

© **Copyright 2023 by Kyo Itakura (Independently published) - All rights reserved.**

The content contained within this book may not be reproduced, duplicated, or transmitted without direct written permission from the author or the publisher.

Under no circumstances will any blame or legal responsibility be held against the publisher, or author, for any damages, reparation, or monetary loss due to the information contained within this book, either directly or indirectly.

Legal Notice:

This book is copyright protected. It is only for personal use. You cannot amend, distribute, sell, use, quote, or paraphrase any part, or the content within this book, without the author's or publisher's consent.

Disclaimer Notice:

Please note that the information in this document is for educational and entertainment purposes only. All effort has been executed to present accurate, up-to-date, reliable, and complete information. No warranties of any kind are declared or implied. Readers acknowledge that the author is not engaging in the rendering of legal, financial, medical, or professional advice. The content within this book has been derived from various sources. Please consult a licensed professional before attempting any techniques outlined in this book.

By reading this document, the reader agrees that under no circumstances is the author responsible for any direct or indirect losses incurred due to the use of the information contained within this document, including, but not limited to, errors, omissions, or inaccuracies.

Contents

Introduction   1

1. Chapter 1: Understanding Bonsai   3
   The History of Bonsai
   The Concept of Wabi-Sabi
   The Symbolism of Bonsai
   Benefits of Practicing Bonsai

2. Chapter 2: Choosing and Caring for Bonsai Trees   14
   Popular Tree Species for Bonsai Beginners
   Fundamentals of Bonsai Care

3. Chapter 3: Essential Tools, Techniques, and Training   25
   Tools of the Trade
   Bonsai Training and Manipulation
   How to Prune Your Bonsai Tree
   Wiring Your Bonsai Tree

4. Chapter 4: Styling and Designing Bonsai 36
   Traditional Bonsai Styles
   Contemporary Bonsai Styles
   Balance and Harmony in Bonsai Styling
   How Bonsai Proportions Are Determined

5. Chapter 5: Bonsai Pot Selection and Display 48
   Bonsai Pots: The Art of Style and Use
   Categories of Bonsai Pots
   The Art of Positioning and Display
   Color Harmony

6. Chapter 6: Bonsai Care and Maintenance 60
   Seasonal Care for Bonsai Trees
   Winter Hibernation
   Spring Growth
   Summer Dormancy
   Autumn Decline and Renewal
   Pest and Disease Control
   How to Water Your Bonsai Tree
   Repotting
   The Perfect Bonsai Soil

7. Chapter 7: Advanced Bonsai Techniques 71
   Air-Layering
   Grafting in Bonsai

    Performing Approach Grafting
    Performing Thread Grafting
    Performing Scion Grafting

8. Chapter 8: Bonsai Exhibition and Future Journey   84

    Preparing Your Bonsai for Exhibition

    Judgment Criteria for Bonsai Exhibitions

Conclusion   91

References   93

Introduction

Bonsai, the time-honored art of cultivating miniature trees, has captivated the hearts and minds of enthusiasts for centuries. With its origins deeply rooted in East Asia, Bonsai embodies a harmonious blend of nature and human creativity. This book serves as a comprehensive guide to unlocking the secrets behind this intricate practice, offering invaluable insights into the history, techniques, and philosophy that underpin the world of Bonsai. Each step in the Bonsai journey is meticulously explored, from selecting the perfect specimen to shaping its delicate branches with precision.

Delving into the profound connection between Bonsai and spirituality, this book illuminates how cultivating these living sculptures can foster a sense of tranquility and mindfulness in our fast-paced modern lives. We will also explore Bonsai's various styles and aesthetics, showcasing the diversity and creativity that can be achieved within this art form.

Furthermore, the book provides practical advice on caring for Bonsai trees, including watering, fertilizing, and pest control techniques. It emphasizes the importance of patience and dedication in nurturing these miniature masterpieces. It outlines how to achieve the most authentic Bonsai experience by selecting the right tree species, shaping it through careful pruning and wiring, and creating a harmonious balance between the tree and its container.

Whether you are a seasoned enthusiast or just beginning to explore this enchanting world of miniature trees, this book is a feast for the eyes and a source of inspiration for anyone seeking to bring a touch of natural elegance into their lives. From the delicate curves of the branches to the intricate patterns of the leaves, every detail is a testament to the skill and dedication of the artist who created them.

The art of Bonsai is a true testament to the beauty that can be achieved through patience and attention to detail. They serve as a reminder of the beauty that can be found in nature and inspire us to cultivate our own sense of artistry in our lives. So, if you're ready to discover the many wonders of this ancient art, pick up your tools, find your tree, and embark on this enchanting journey of Bonsai – where artistry meets nature and life intertwines with beauty.

Chapter One

Chapter 1: Understanding Bonsai

The ancient art of Bonsai is known for its delicate yet beautiful appearance and diverse nature. Despite the care and sometimes obsession, that is put into the creation of this art form, it is not really understood or even known by as many people as you would think. Bonsai has been practiced throughout history, from China to Japan and modern-day America. At its core, it is a discipline where art meets science, taking a small tree and making it seem larger than life through artistic techniques and clever cultivation methods. Bonsai artists meticulously prune and shape the tree's branches and roots, using specialized tools to create a harmonious balance between its form and container. The artistry lies in capturing nature's essence in miniature, evoking a sense of contentment and unity. Each Bonsai tree tells a unique story, reflecting the artist's vision and interpretation of nature's beauty. It is a testament to patience and dedication, as it can take years, even decades, for a Bonsai tree to reach its full potential. Creating Bonsai is an expression of art and science, a fusion of creativity and precision. It is nature's infinite splendor and beauty wrapped in a little package.

The History of Bonsai

Bonsai was born in China, where it was originally known as penzai or punsai. By 700 AD, the Chinese had developed the practice of 'pun-sai,' or growing miniature trees in containers, employing unique procedures. Initially, only the most affluent members of society performed pun-tsai using native-collected specimens, and the trees were sent as luxury gifts across China. However, it soon spread to Japan during the Kamakura era, where it evolved into what we now recognize as Bonsai.

The Japanese embraced this art form and infused it with their own cultural sensibilities, giving rise to unique styles such as formal upright, informal upright, cascade, and windswept. Bonsai soon became not just a hobby but a way of life for many enthusiasts who dedicated themselves to perfecting the techniques required for its creation and maintenance. Today, it has gained global popularity, captivating people with its intricate beauty and profound symbolism. It is seen as a meditative practice that encourages patience, discipline, and an appreciation for the delicate balance between nature and human intervention. As Bonsai continues to evolve and inspire generations of artists, its timeless allure remains a testament to the enduring power of nature and the human spirit.

The art of Bonsai has transcended cultures and generations and has become a sincerely important part of the human experience. It inspires people to learn more about their environment, to appreciate the natural world, and to grow in appreciation and understanding for one another. It represents the beauty of nature at its most sublime, with each bonsai tree being a world unto itself.

The art of Bonsai is not just about shaping and pruning trees; it is a profound expression of our connection to the earth and our desire to harmonize with it. Each Bonsai tree tells a unique story, representing the passage of time and the resilience of nature. It is proof of the power of human creativity and ingenuity and a humbling reminder of our place in the grand tapestry of life. As we continue to delve deeper into the world of Bonsai, exploring new techniques and experimenting with different species, we uncover endless possibilities for self-expression and artistic exploration. The beauty lies in the final result and the journey itself—the hours spent carefully tending to each branch, shaping each leaf, and nurturing each root.

Bonsai teaches us patience, reminding us that true mastery cannot be rushed but must be cultivated over time. It teaches us discipline as we learn to make difficult decisions about which branches to prune and which to keep. It also teaches us respect for nature as we develop a deep understanding and appreciation for the delicate balance required to maintain the health and beauty of these miniature trees. It demonstrates the human spirit as artists strive to reach new heights of artistic expression and technical expertise.

The Concept of Wabi-Sabi

In Japanese, Wabi-Sabi is described as the beauty that results from the natural cycles of growth, decay, renewal, and transformation. Its focus on impermanence encourages us to appreciate what we have in the present moment instead of worrying about what we may lose or gain in the future. This philosophy is deeply intertwined with the practice of Bonsai, as each tree represents the passage of time and the ever-changing nature of life itself. The art of Bonsai teaches us to find beauty in imperfection and to embrace the unique characteristics and quirks that make each tree special. It reminds us that nothing lasts forever and that there is a certain elegance in the fleeting moments of life.

As we meticulously prune and shape our Bonsai trees, we are reminded of our own need for growth and transformation. Bonsai encourages us to slow down, be patient, and be attentive to the subtle changes that occur over time. It teaches us to appreciate the small things in life and to find joy in the delicate balance between control and surrender. The complex branches and meticulously designed foliage showcase the beauty of nature's intricacies. In a world that often feels chaotic and fast-paced, Bonsai provides a much-needed escape, allowing us to connect with nature on a deeper level. It is a practice that requires dedication, discipline, and an understanding of the delicate balance between man and nature. By slowing down and focusing on the present moment, we become more attuned to the world around us and our relationship with it. As we focus on cultivating each Bonsai tree, we also cultivate better versions of ourselves.

The Symbolism of Bonsai

Bonsai trees symbolize time, eternity, prosperity, health, honor, and death. Some say they are a spiritual connection between heaven and man on earth. They signify the collective life force that flows through everything in nature, from the smallest leaf to the largest tree. They are the energy of beauty. When a Bonsai tree is placed in a home, it is believed to bring prosperity and honor. The tree stands for longevity and harmony, reflected in its shape and size.

Bonsai allows you to share your art with others and see them reflect on the beauty of your work as they study every detail and admire your craftsmanship. It is a form of expression that allows you to connect with people profoundly, as they appreciate the time and effort you have put into creating something so intricate and captivating. Bonsai also teaches patience and mindfulness, as you must carefully tend to and shape the tree's needs over time. The nurturing and shaping process mirrors the journey of life, where we, too, must cultivate our own growth and adapt to the changes that come our way. Bonsai is a practice that encourages introspection and self-reflection as you contemplate the beauty of imperfection and find solace in embracing the flaws. As you immerse yourself in this ancient tradition, you become part of a lineage that stretches back centuries, connecting you to countless individuals who have found comfort and inspiration in these miniature masterpieces.

Bonsai is a powerful form of art that transcends the traditional art forms of painting and sculpture. It combines the practical craftsmanship taught in woodworking with the transcendental beauty of traditional Zen art forms. According to Zen philosophy, nature is a reflection of heaven on earth; the Bonsai artist seeks to capture this essence and create a living representation of the natural world in miniature. Each Bonsai tree is meticulously shaped and pruned, with every branch and leaf carefully considered to evoke a sense of harmony and balance. The process requires patience and dedication, as the artist must work with the tree's natural growth patterns, coaxing it into a desired form over time. As the Bonsai matures, it begins to take on a life of its own, becoming a visual representation of the artist's inner spirit.

Beyond its aesthetic appeal, Bonsai also holds deep spiritual significance. It is believed that tending to these miniature trees cultivates mindfulness and presence, allowing one to connect with the rhythm of nature and find inner peace. The art of Bonsai is not merely about creating beautiful objects; it is an expression of reverence, honor, and appreciation. It demonstrates the importance of nurturing what we already have and celebrating the fleeting beauty found only in the present moment. Through Bonsai, we become part of a long tradition of those who have found peace in the natural world, and we come to know that there is a certain wisdom to be found between the branches of a tree.

Anyone with a love for nature and a willingness to spend hours shaping and pruning can do a Bonsai. It is also delightful for children, who can learn patience and creativity as they play with their Bonsai tree. People of all ages and walks of life can appreciate the enigmatic beauty that bonsai trees bring to the world. Hundreds of species of Bonsai trees can be sculpted into various shapes and sizes, allowing for a huge range of creative possibilities. Bonsai is an art form that anyone can enjoy, regardless of their artistic background or skill level. If you can take care of a house plant, you can take care of a Bonsai tree easily. From the beginner with little experience in gardening to the experienced artist with years of experience, there is an artistry and depth to Bonsai that is accessible to everyone.

Benefits of Practicing Bonsai

Many different types of Bonsai trees provide a refreshing change from the everyday routine. Some enthusiasts will tell you that the practice helps them relax, deepen their creative thinking, and provide a sense of calmness, which is all true, but there's more, so much more. Here is a list of all you stand to gain from practicing Bonsai:

- Bonsai trees provide a sense of accomplishment as you grow and care for your tree over time. Through this process, you learn patience and mindfulness, two essential life skills. It also encourages you to create something of beauty through your everyday efforts and builds self-esteem through a creative practice that has value beyond the material.

- It is an opportunity to connect with nature on a purely sensory level and see the world through a new lens. The study of Bonsai will lead you to appreciate the complexity and beauty of nature, both on a large and small scale. It teaches you to observe nature around you with renewed inspiration so that all your interactions with nature reflect your newfound sense of awe.

- Bonsai is a chance for introspection and self-reflection as you contemplate the beauty of imperfection and find solace in embracing the flaws. Through the art of Bonsai, you learn to accept that life is not always perfect, just like the twisted branches and gnarled trunks of these miniature trees. It teaches you patience and resilience as you carefully shape and prune each branch, knowing that growth takes time and effort. Nurturing a Bonsai tree can be meditative, allowing you to escape from the hustle and bustle of everyday life. As you immerse yourself in this ancient practice, you begin to understand the interconnectedness of all living things. It reminds us that we are part of a larger ecosystem where every action we take impacts the world around us. It encourages us to tread lightly on this earth and cherish its beauty. In a world filled with constant distractions, Bonsai offers a sanctuary where we can reconnect with ourselves and nature.

- Tending to your Bonsai tree is a way to relax and unwind. While working with a Bonsai tree, you are actively caring for something living and breathing, so your mind is occupied with the practical aspects of caretaking, such as watering, pruning, and shaping. This focused attention allows you to temporarily let go of any worries or issues weighing you down. As you delicately trim the branches and gently shape the foliage, you become fully present in the moment and attuned to the subtle needs of your Bonsai. The rhythmic flow of this activity calms your soul, and you are immersed in a soothing state of mind. It is an excellent way to de-stress after a long day at work or school.

- Bonsai serves as a powerful reminder of our connection to nature. In a world dominated by technology and urban landscapes, it is easy to forget the importance of nature. The simple act of tending to a Bonsai tree can remind us that nature is a powerful moving and breathing force, and we are part of it. Realizing that humans are just one tiny piece of the natural world can be humbling. We are a wild species, just like all the other animals and plants, full of instinct and beauty. Through the art of Bonsai, we come to understand our place in the scheme of things and find a sense of peace in this delicate balance between order and chaos.

- Fostering creativity in children is important for their cognitive development and self-esteem. One way to jumpstart a child's creativity is by introducing them to Bonsai trees early on in life when they are less likely to be overwhelmed by complex artistic concepts. Bonsai can spark an interest in gardening and encourage curiosity about how different plants can be used for various purposes. It is also a great way for parents to spend time with their children and foster bonding. Through the process of tending to your Bonsai trees, you can teach your child about patience, responsibility, and mindfulness.

The art of Bonsai is a beautiful practice that can stimulate your senses and refine your appreciation for the natural world. It encourages mindfulness, creative thinking, and gratitude for nature. It fosters a sense of self-worth through an act of creation characterized by flow and tranquility. In an increasingly busy world, Bonsai offers a much-needed sanctuary where you can reenergize and find peace within yourself. By carefully tending to the miniature trees, shaping and pruning them with precision, you become intimately connected with nature's cycles and the beauty of growth and transformation. The art of Bonsai teaches patience and perseverance as you watch your creation evolve, reminding you to embrace the process rather than focusing solely on the result. It highlights the importance of simplifying your life and living in the moment, freed from the distractions of technology and constant stimulation.

Chapter Two

Chapter 2: Choosing and Caring for Bonsai Trees

Bonsai trees might not be the easiest thing to find at your local nursery, but they're worth a bit of a trek if you want to take care of one. Some people might not know how to choose a Bonsai tree, or even if they've decided on something, they might not be sure how best to care for it. First, you should know that some general characteristics make a tree suitable for Bonsai. These include size, foliage, growth patterns, and disease issues like insect infestation or a damaged trunk.

Size

Bonsai trees are generally kept in small containers, and this can make the choice of tree a bit difficult. You'll want to look for a tree that naturally stays small or can be easily pruned and shaped to maintain a compact size. Some popular choices for Bonsai include Japanese maple, juniper, and pine trees. These trees have naturally small leaves and branches, making them ideal for creating the intricate and delicate designs Bonsai is known for. Additionally, their growth patterns lend themselves well to the art of Bonsai, as they can be trained and shaped into various styles like the cascade, formal upright, or windswept.

Foliage

The foliage of a Bonsai tree is another important characteristic to consider. You'll want to choose a tree with leaves that are proportionate to its size and appealing color and texture. Look for trees with dense, fine leaves that can be easily trimmed and styled. Trees with exciting leaf shapes or colors can also add visual interest to your Bonsai collection. Different species of trees offer a wide range of foliage options, from the Japanese maple's vibrant red leaves to the pine tree's soft needles. It's important to select a tree with foliage that complements the overall design and aesthetic you're aiming for in your Bonsai creation.

Pests and Diseases

Bonsai trees are not immune to common issues like insect infestation or damage to their trunks. Recognizing and treating these problems is an indispensable part of Bonsai care. If you want to purchase a Bonsai tree, look over the entire tree carefully for signs of insect infestation, such as small holes in the leaves or branches or discoloration on the trunk. Damaged trunks can cause the tree to lose its shape and symmetry, so you should be careful to avoid buying a tree that is already damaged.

Growth Patterns

Bonsai trees are known for their unique and artistic shapes, achieved through careful pruning and training. Some trees naturally have more desirable growth patterns for Bonsai, such as the cascading branches of a Juniper or the twisted trunk of a Ficus. Regardless, you should consider the natural growth habits of the tree you choose and how it can be manipulated to create the desired aesthetic effect. Understanding the growth patterns of different tree species can help determine the level of maintenance required to maintain the desired shape. For example, trees with fast-growing branches may need more frequent pruning to keep them in check, while slower-growing trees may require less frequent maintenance. By selecting a tree with a growth pattern that aligns with your vision for the Bonsai, you can create a harmonious and balanced composition that will continue to evolve and mature over time.

Popular Tree Species for Bonsai Beginners

If you're looking for a tree for your first bonsai project, these species are popular for beginners.

Juniper

The juniper is ideal for those seeking a more rugged and resilient Bonsai tree. The juniper species is one of the most popular trees used for Bonsai. Junipers are hardy plants that can adapt to many difficult conditions. They are native to high elevations and can thrive in different climates, making them an ideal option for Bonsai beginners with less experience growing plants in their area. They have tiny needles that grow in bunches and range in color from grayish-green to bluish-green, sometimes with a silvery hue. Juniper Bonsai are attractive trees known for their bright foliage color and needled branches that refine well with pruning techniques.

Pine

Pines are popular Bonsai trees because of their large, lightweight cones that create unique shapes and designs. They are known for their black needles, which grow in whorls around the branches and are soft to the touch. Pines can be easily pruned for refinement and are versatile trees that add a natural, organic element to any Bonsai garden. The Scots pine is one of the most popular pines used for Bonsai because of its rugged appearance and ability to withstand harsh weather conditions. Its bark has a beautiful reddish-brown color that adds depth and texture to the overall aesthetic of the tree. Another popular pine for Bonsai is the Japanese black pine, known for its distinctive twisted trunk and elegant silhouette. This pine species requires careful pruning and wiring to achieve the desired shape, but the result is a stunning Bonsai with intricate branch structure and delicate foliage. Lastly, the Mugo pine is a compact variety perfect for smaller Bonsai gardens or indoor cultivation. Its dense foliage and compact size makes it easy to maintain and shape while providing a vibrant greenery burst. Overall, pines are an excellent choice for Bonsai enthusiasts looking to add diversity and visual interest to their collections.

Ficus

Ficus trees, or fig trees, are popular for indoor bonsai enthusiasts. These trees have smooth, shiny leaves that are typically dark green. Ficus Bonsai trees are known for their ability to adapt to different environments and thrive in bright and low-light conditions. They are also relatively easy to care for, making them an excellent option for beginners. These trees can be shaped into various styles, such as the formal upright or the informal cascade, allowing bonsai enthusiasts to showcase their creativity. With proper care and maintenance, Ficus bonsai trees can live for many years, creating a beautiful and long-lived addition to your garden.

Chinese Elm

Chinese elms are popular Bonsai trees found in nearly all collections. They're known for their vibrant green leaves, which tend to change colors during different seasons. The leaves turn an apple-green color during the spring, summer, and fall, while in winter, they darken to a deep emerald shade. Chinese elms have a naturally compact appearance and tend to grow slower than other types of trees used for Bonsai. They have a graceful and elegant branching structure with small leaves that create a delicate and refined aesthetic. Chinese elms are also highly adaptable and can tolerate a wide range of conditions, making them suitable for indoor and outdoor cultivation. Proper care and pruning allow these Bonsai trees to develop intricate branch patterns and a stunning year-round display of bright foliage.

Rosemary

Rosemary is native to the Mediterranean and is commonly used as an indoor Bonsai, but it can also be grown outdoors in warm climates. Rosemary Bonsai trees are popular because they produce fragrant white flowers in spring and summer. They have needle-like leaves that grow in clusters along the branches and their trunks, typically gray or pale green, adding a unique charm to the overall aesthetic of the Bonsai. The compact nature of Rosemary Bonsai trees makes them perfect for small spaces, like an apartment or office. Their slow growth rate allows for easy maintenance and shaping, making them ideal for beginners in the art of Bonsai. In addition to their visual appeal, rosemary bonsai trees also offer practical benefits. The leaves of the rosemary plant are known for their aromatic fragrance and flavor. Having a Rosemary Bonsai tree not only adds beauty to your space but also provides you with fresh herbs that can give your cooking a spicy boost. Whether you keep it indoors or outdoors, a Rosemary Bonsai tree will surely bring joy and functionality to any environment.

Cherry Blossom

The cherry blossom Bonsai tree is a perfect choice for those looking for a more delicate and graceful option. These trees are admired for their stunning pink or white blossoms that bloom in early spring. The cherry blossom Bonsai has small, oval-shaped leaves that turn vibrant shades of red and orange in the fall, creating a breathtaking display of colors against the backdrop of its smooth, dark bark. Its branches gracefully curve and twist, giving it an elegant and whimsical appearance. The cherry blossom Bonsai tree symbolizes beauty, love, and the transient nature of life, making it a meaningful and symbolic addition to any space.

Maple

The maple Bonsai is an excellent choice if you prefer a Bonsai tree with vibrant foliage throughout the year. Known for its stunning autumn colors, the maple bonsai showcases leaves in shades of fiery reds, oranges, and yellows that create a mesmerizing spectacle. The maple Bonsai boasts lush green leaves in spring and summer, providing a refreshing burst of color. Its distinctive trunk features unique patterns and textures that add depth and character to its appeal.

Cotoneaster

Cotoneaster is a popular arid-climate bonsai tree, which means it can be used as a Bonsai tree for beginners in any location. This type of plant is known for its dense foliage, which can be green or blue-green and often displays shades of purple. Cotoneaster foliage requires little pruning and tends to naturally prune itself without needing additional help from you. Its small leaves create a delicate and elegant appearance, making it a favorite among Bonsai enthusiasts. The tree produces small white or pink flowers in the spring and bright red berries in the fall, adding a splash of color to your bonsai display.

Fundamentals of Bonsai Care

Once you've chosen the proper tree for your bonsai project, it's time to start caring for it. This is where the fun begins! Even though bonsai enthusiasts often consider the art of Bonsai a complicated process, the truth is that bonsai trees are relatively simple to care for and can be enjoyed by even the most inexperienced gardeners. With the proper knowledge and techniques, anyone can successfully care for a bonsai tree. You need to understand the specific needs of your Bonsai tree, such as its watering, fertilizing, and pruning requirements. Providing the proper amount of sunlight and temperature is also crucial for the tree's health. Regularly checking for pests and diseases and taking appropriate measures to prevent or treat them is another essential. By following these fundamental care practices, even beginners can create a thriving and beautiful Bonsai tree.

Watering

Bonsai trees require regular but careful watering to maintain their health. Watering the tree thoroughly ensures that the water reaches all parts of the soil, but avoiding overwatering is critical to curbing root rot. A good practice is to check the soil's moisture level by inserting a finger about an inch deep into the soil. If it feels dry, it's time to water the Bonsai tree. It is best to use a gentle stream of water, preferably from a watering can or a misting bottle, to prevent soil erosion and damage to the delicate roots. It is also important to water the tree evenly, ensuring all areas of the soil receive moisture. However, be careful not to flood the pot or leave the tree sitting in standing water, as this can suffocate the roots and cause harm to the tree. Additionally, avoid watering during the hottest part of the day because this will cause rapid evaporation and may not allow the tree enough time to absorb water properly. Instead, water in the morning or evening when temperatures are cooler, and there is less chance of water loss due to evaporation. By following these watering guidelines and paying close attention to the moisture needs of your Bonsai tree, you can ensure its health and longevity.

Fertilizing

When choosing the right blend of nutrients for your Bonsai tree, a variety of options will work well, depending on your tree's specific needs. Since Bonsai trees are small in size and design, they have a limited number of nutrients they can absorb and utilize from the soil. Therefore, you must take great care in selecting a mix that will provide the correct balance of nutrients. Every fertilizer has three fundamental elements: nitrogen, phosphorus, and potassium (NPK). Nitrogen is necessary for healthy plant development. Phosphorus is essential for strong cell walls and root growth, while potassium helps promote healthy foliage growth. Beyond these three elements, trace elements contribute to healthy foliage and blossoms, like boron, magnesium, iron, zinc, and copper. Thankfully, today it's possible to choose a fertilizer containing the complete nutrients necessary to help your Bonsai tree thrive.

Different NPK ratios are frequently used by growers depending on the trees and time of year. Experts, on the other hand, are increasingly advising utilizing the same NPK ratio throughout the Bonsai growth cycle because most Bonsai trees need fertilizer during the whole growth season, from early spring to mid-fall. However, depending on the type, season, growth stage, and tree health, you might have to tweak the feeding regime slightly.

The growth stage of your trees plays a key role in the fertilizer you use. Strong growth is what we want for a Bonsai in its early stages of development, so we need a relatively powerful fertilizer, but for a mature and balanced tree, less is better. Depending on the fertilizer you purchase, you may use different amounts and apply it at various intervals, but make sure to feed your Bonsai according to the directions on the fertilizer container.

Lighting

Even though Bonsai trees are pretty small in size, they still need adequate lighting to produce healthy foliage and flowers. When selecting a tree for your bonsai garden, there are several things to consider regarding the amount of sunlight it will receive. Factors such as where you live, the time of year, and the style of your garden can all affect how much light will reach your plants. While it is difficult to predict precisely how much light your tree will get, you can best approximate the amount of sun it will receive by adjusting the location and style of your display. A south-facing window is the perfect environment for Bonsai plants, but you may need a timer to control light exposure throughout the day.

A good rule of thumb is to avoid placing Bonsai trees in full sunlight for more than 10 hours a day because you will be dealing with sunburn and damage to the delicate foliage. Instead, you can opt for a spot that receives partial shade, especially during the day's hottest hours. This will provide your Bonsai tree with a balance of sunlight and shade, allowing it to thrive without being overwhelmed by intense heat. You should also consider the time of year when positioning your tree. During the summer, when the sun is at its strongest, it may be necessary to set up some additional shade or protection for your Bonsai. You can achieve this by placing it under a pergola or using a shade cloth to filter the sunlight. On the other hand, during the winter months, when sunlight is limited, you may need to relocate your Bonsai to a sunnier spot or consider using artificial grow lights to supplement its light requirements. By carefully considering these factors and adjusting accordingly, you can ensure that your Bonsai tree receives just the right amount of sunlight for healthy growth.

Chapter Three

Chapter 3: Essential Tools, Techniques, and Training

Bonsai maintenance is about more than just watering and fertilizing your little tree. It's also about ensuring your tree is safe, healthy, and strong to thrive and grow. This involves regular pruning to maintain its desired shape and size and wiring and shaping to create the desired aesthetic. To keep your tree alive and healthy, you must understand the basics of bonsai maintenance, so here's a quick rundown of the essential tools and techniques you need to know.

Tools of the Trade

The tools you need for bonsai training and maintenance are pretty basic. You don't need a professional setup, but you will need to invest a little bit of money into the basics. Here's what you need:

1. **Bonsai Shears for Pruning and Trimming Branches:** These specialized shears are designed to make clean and precise cuts, allowing you to shape and maintain the desired structure of your bonsai tree. Investing in a high-quality pair that fits comfortably in your hand and has sharp blades for efficient pruning is essential.

2. **Concave Cutters for Branch Removal**: These unique cutters have a curved blade that creates a concave cut, which helps with quicker healing and reduces scarring on the tree. They are essential for removing larger branches without damaging the bonsai's overall design.

3. **Wire Cutters for Shaping**: Wiring is a common technique used in bonsai to guide the growth of branches and create desired shapes, so wire cutters are necessary for safely removing the wire without causing any harm to the tree.

4. **Bonsai Wire for Shaping Branches**: Bonsai wire is essential for shaping branches and directing tree growth. It allows the bonsai artist to carefully wrap and bend branches, encouraging them to grow in a specific direction. The wire should be chosen based on the size and flexibility of the branch, ensuring that it provides enough support without causing any damage. With proper use of bonsai wire, intricate and artistic shapes can be achieved, adding beauty and elegance to the bon-

sai tree.

5. **Pliers:** Pliers are essential for bending and securing the wire in place. They provide the necessary grip and leverage to carefully shape the branches without causing any harm. With a firm hold on the wire, the bonsai artist can gently manipulate it to create graceful curves or precise angles. The pliers also come in handy for securing the wire tightly, ensuring it stays in place as the branch grows and develops. You can easily create complex, sculptural shapes by using pliers in conjunction with bonsai wire.

6. **A Bonsai Pot**: A bonsai pot for your plant is another crucial element in the art of bonsai. These pots are specifically designed to enhance the appeal of the tree and complement its size and style. They come in various shapes, sizes, and materials, such as ceramic, clay, or even stone. The choice of a bonsai pot should consider factors like the tree's age, species, and desired visual impact. A well-chosen pot can elevate the presentation of the bonsai, creating a harmonious balance between the tree and its container. It adds a sense of refinement and sophistication to the overall composition, making it truly captivating. On top of that, bonsai pots also provide practical benefits like proper drainage and root development. These play a vital role in maintaining the health and longevity of your bonsai tree by ensuring op-

timal growing conditions. So, when choosing a bonsai pot for your plant, take your time to find one that will enhance its beauty and enrich its health over the long term.

7. **Repotting Supplies**: When you repot a bonsai, you need to avoid breaking the roots, so it's best to invest in tools to help you ensure this doesn't happen. Repotting tools such as root hooks and root rakes are essential for gently untangling and pruning the roots without causing damage. These tools allow you to carefully remove the tree from its current pot, trim any excess roots, and create a suitable environment for new growth. Moreover, they also help preserve the prized shape of the bonsai tree during the repotting process, allowing it to recover fully after re-establishment.

8. **Watering Can with a Fine Nozzle**: A watering can with a fine nozzle is an essential tool for precisely watering your bonsai tree. The fine nozzle allows you to control the water flow, ensuring it reaches the roots without causing any damage. This is particularly important as bonsai trees have delicate root systems that can easily be overwatered or underwatered. Using a watering can with a fine nozzle, you can carefully and accurately water your bonsai tree, providing it with the right amount of moisture it needs for healthy growth. The fine nozzle also helps to prevent water from splashing onto the foliage, reducing the risk of

fungal diseases and blistering.

9. **Humidity Tray:** A humidity tray is a shallow water-filled tray placed beneath the bonsai tree. As the water evaporates, the humidity around the tree increases, which is good for its growth and hydration. The tray also acts as a decorative element, adding to the visual appeal of your bonsai display. The water level in the tray should be monitored regularly to ensure it doesn't dry out. The tray size should also be considered, as larger trees require a deeper tray for proper hydration.

10. **Moisture Meter:** Bonsai enthusiasts need a moisture meter to gauge the soil's moisture content precisely. This should not be overlooked because your bonsai tree's health can suffer from overwatering or underwatering. By sticking the moisture meter into the soil, you can determine whether your tree needs to be watered or has enough moisture. This eliminates any guesswork and guarantees that you provide your bonsai with the ideal amount of water for its particular needs. Using a moisture meter, you can keep a healthy balance and save yourself potential trouble from ineffective watering techniques. It is a practical and dependable tool that each bonsai owner should have.

Bonsai Training and Manipulation

A bonsai is a living thing and requires constant care and effort to keep it looking as good as possible. Whether you are a professional bonsai artist or just starting, you need a good understanding of the art of bonsai manipulation and training. Bonsai training involves shaping and styling the tree to create a specific look. This can be done through techniques like wiring, pruning, and defoliation. By carefully manipulating the branches and foliage, you can create a bonsai tree that looks significantly different from the one you started with. Training also helps maintain the tree's size and proportions, ensuring it remains in scale with its container. This process requires patience—and plenty of it. It requires consistency and precision, dedication to the art form, and the understanding that missteps may result in the loss of your tree or a deviation from what you had intended.

Apical dominance, one of the fundamental concepts to grasp in bonsai training, refers to the natural tendency of the tree's main apex to grow stronger and faster than the lateral branches. So, by selectively pruning and wiring the branches, you can redirect the tree's energy and encourage more balanced growth. This also involves carefully removing or shortening the dominant apex while encouraging the development of weaker branches. By doing this, you essentially create the illusion of an equally balanced canopy. This is one of the most common practices in bonsai tree training. It's also a good tip to create a more aged and gnarled tree that looks like it's been growing for decades.

Another important aspect of bonsai training is defoliation. This technique involves removing a portion or all of the leaves from the tree. Defoliation serves several purposes in bonsai cultivation. First, it helps reduce leaf size, which is crucial for maintaining proper proportions in miniature trees. Secondly, defoliation can stimulate new growth and encourage ramification, creating a more intricate branch structure. Lastly, it allows for better observation of the tree's overall form and structure, making it easier to identify areas that require further training or refinement.

How to Prune Your Bonsai Tree

Pruning is the art of trimming or removing branches from the bonsai tree to encourage healthy growth and give it a certain aesthetic appeal. Ideally, you should prune your bonsai tree a few times per year. These trimming sessions can be divided into corrective pruning and all-around maintenance pruning. Corrective pruning involves removing dead and diseased branches, while all-around maintenance pruning involves shaping and refining the design of your bonsai tree as it grows. It can be challenging to decide which branches should be left and which should be cut off, not only because it is irreversible but also because it affects how the tree will look as it matures. Thankfully, there is a surefire way to do it right. These steps will guide you as you prune your bonsai:

Step 1: Examine the Tree

Before you start pruning your bonsai, make sure to examine it closely. Check for dead or diseased branches and remove them carefully. Remove any parts of the tree that disease or pests have damaged, like fungal growth or insect infestation. This will prevent the spread of infection and ensure your bonsai tree grows clean and disease-free. Also, look for branches growing in the wrong direction or otherwise positioned awkwardly. These branches should be removed because they can cause damage to your bonsai and detract from the look you are going for.

Step 2: Sever with Care

Now that you have examined your tree, it's time to prune it. The key to pruning is severing the branch with a clean cut. This will reduce the chances of infection and help the tree heal faster. Make sure to trim branches at their base, where they have a larger mass that makes them less likely to break than further up the stem. It is also important to avoid trimming too much off at any one time, as this can shock your tree and cause it to rapidly lose or gain moisture, leading to problems you don't want and even death in some instances.

Step 3: Trim the Trunk

After you have pruned the branches, you can move on to trunk trimming. The trunk is like a tree's foundation and should be left intact. However, there are some circumstances where it may need to be trimmed or shaped to make it more appealing. For example, if the trunk has branches growing out of it that you want to keep, trim just above it so it doesn't die due to a lack of sunlight or nutrients. You can also trim branches growing on the bark to change the tree's overall shape.

The goal of bonsai pruning is to shape and refine your tree's design and to get the most out of the branches that you have. Trim your tree regularly so you have a strong, healthy trunk and a lively canopy. Aim for balance. If one branch is out of proportion with the rest, trim it until it matches its neighbors. Think of your tree as an intricate puzzle you can't solve until all the pieces are trimmed to perfection.

Wiring Your Bonsai Tree

Wiring is a technique that involves tying branches into a specific position to shape them. This technique can be described as the "art of movement" and creates an organic-looking bonsai tree with an interesting shape and visual appeal. It is an art form that requires practice, patience, and skill, but each can be developed with experience. The many benefits of proper wiring include creating a more three-dimensional design while also ensuring lower branch attachment and a more robust trunk. Even better, wiring can guide and direct the direction of your tree, especially when you are unsure where it will go.

You will need annealed copper or anodized aluminum wire, which you can get from a hardware or electronics store. Some bonsai enthusiasts prefer to use annealed copper wire, which is more expensive but easier to work with. Aluminum wire is cheaper and easier to find but can damage your bonsai tree if not appropriately handled. While you can start with a thin gauge of wire if you're new to the technique, experts recommend using a thicker gauge of wire that is easier to manipulate and gives you a stronger hold.

After you have gathered your materials and laid them out, inspect each branch carefully to determine which ones you should wire. You want to only focus on the branches that are out of place. Trying to correct everything at once could overwhelm you, and your tree might not develop as you envisioned it. Look for branches growing in the wrong direction or at an awkward angle with other branches. Also, pay attention to each branch's length, thickness, and location relative to the rest of the canopy. Ensure they still fulfill their role in the tree's design, even after being positioned properly. Wire basic branches first, then move on to more challenging branches.

After you have looked through your tree and determined what branches you want to wire, there are two basic wiring techniques: double wiring and single wiring. Double wiring involves wiring two branches of similar thickness that are close to one another. This will emphasize the natural movement you are trying to create and make adjusting easier. Single wiring is done on a branch with a thinner, more flexible stem and involves wiring it to a main branch or the trunk.

Before bending the branches, wire every branch you intend to shape. When wiring a whole tree, start with the trunk and work your way up to the primary branches before moving on to the secondary branches. As a rule of thumb, use wire 1/3 the thickness of the branch you are wiring. This is because the wire needs to be thick enough to keep the branch in place but not so thick that it damages or cuts into the branch.

Begin by wrapping the wire around the base of the branch and then gently guiding it along the length, making sure to space the wire coils evenly. As you wrap, be careful not to apply too much pressure to avoid causing breakage or strain on the branch. Once you reach the tip of the branch, secure the wire by twisting it back onto itself or using wire cutters to create a loop. Repeat this process for each branch you wish to shape, ensuring that you maintain a balanced and aesthetically pleasing form. Remember to adjust and reposition the wire over time to accommodate growth and prevent constriction. With patience and practice, your wired branches will gradually take on the desired shape, creating the bonsai of your dreams.

Chapter Four

Chapter 4: Styling and Designing Bonsai

A bonsai tree is a living sculpture that takes years or decades to develop and involves the styling techniques of pruning, trimming, wiring, and shaping to create a miniature representation of nature. The importance of styling and design in bonsai cannot be overstated, as it is the key to achieving balance, harmony, and aesthetic appeal in these small yet captivating trees. Through careful pruning, branches are strategically removed to enhance the tree's overall structure and create a sense of proportion. Trimming is another crucial technique that helps maintain the desired size and shape of the foliage, ensuring that the bonsai remains visually pleasing. Wiring plays a vital role in bending and positioning branches, allowing for artistic manipulation and creating dynamic forms. Finally, shaping is where true artistry comes into play, as skilled bonsai enthusiasts carefully sculpt their trees into unique shapes that evoke a sense of Zen and natural beauty. By understanding and applying these styling techniques, bonsai artists can transform ordinary trees into extraordinary works of living art that captivate viewers with their elegance and grace.

The art of growing bonsai does not end with the development of foliage. It should be fun to style and design bonsai. It is a delicate dance between nature and human interference, where the artist must respect the tree's natural growth patterns while guiding it toward their artistic vision. The result is a living masterpiece that brings nature and art together.

Bonsai styling is a continuous journey of learning and experimentation, with each tree presenting its own unique challenges and opportunities for artistic expression. From selecting the right tree species to understanding its specific needs, the bonsai artist must immerse themselves in the worlds of horticulture and botany. They must study the tree's growth habits, response to different pruning techniques, and preferred soil and watering conditions. Once armed with this knowledge, the artist carefully begins the process of shaping the bonsai, and there are many styles to choose from.

Traditional Bonsai Styles

The process of styling bonsai trees is full of artistic considerations, which is why the art form seems so difficult to master. There are three main styles of bonsai: formal upright, informal upright, and cascading. These styles are defined by the tree's overall shape and general appearance and are the foundation for countless sub-styles developed worldwide.

1. **Formal Upright**: A formal upright (chokkan) tree has a vertical trunk that is straight and stiff, with little or no taper or movement. The tree's branches are also stiff, with little or no bending. This majestic style of bonsai is often associated with strength and elegance. The careful pruning and training of the branches create a sense of unity and cohesion. The overall effect is a miniature tree standing tall and proud, commanding attention and admiration.

2. **Informal Upright:** In contrast to the formal upright style, the informal upright (moyogi) style embodies a more natural and relaxed appearance. The trunk may have slight curves or bends, giving it a sense of movement and vitality. The branches are arranged in a more irregular pattern, mimicking the asymmetry in nature. This style allows for more creative expression, as each tree can have its own unique character and personality.

3. **Cascading**: The cascading (kengai) style is perhaps the most dramatic and eye-catching of all bonsai styles. In this style, the trunk grows downward in a graceful curve, resembling a tree growing on a cliff or over a waterfall. The branches also cascade downward, creating an illusion of movement and flow. In this style, less importance

is placed on the tree's overall balance and symmetry, and more emphasis is placed on creating a dynamic appearance.

Each bonsai should have unique styling, reflecting the tree's natural growth habits. In fact, some bonsai are capable of creating multiple styles at once. For example, the tree could exhibit cascading characteristics in its trunk and informal upright characteristics in its branches. This adds a sense of dynamism and creativity to every bonsai while also challenging the artist to develop new skills.

Contemporary Bonsai Styles

Contemporary is the latest style to emerge from bonsai and is perhaps the most dramatic in appearance. Think of them as modifications of the traditional styles with a strong sense of movement and dynamism. These bonsai are perfect for those seeking to express their unique artistic vision. Contemporary bonsai features dramatic leaves, flowing branches, wild forms, and whimsical styling. The branches are also less complicated than those of a traditionally styled tree, with less emphasis on symmetry and more emphasis on movement. Some of these styles include:

- **Literati:** This style is characterized by tall, slender trunks that twist and turn elegantly and unpredictably. The branches are sparse, giving the tree a sense of age and wisdom. This style often evokes a sense of mystery and intrigue, as if the tree holds secrets from centuries past.

- **Windswept:** The windswept style captures the essence of a tree enduring strong winds and harsh conditions. The branches are twisted and bent as if shaped by nature's forces. This style often evokes a sense of resilience and strength in the face of adversity. The windswept tree stands tall, its branches reaching out defiantly as if to say, "I have weathered the storm and emerged stronger." It symbolizes perseverance and determination, reminding us that even in the harshest conditions, there is beauty and strength to be found. The twisted branches tell a story of survival; each curve and bend is a testament to the tree's ability to adapt and thrive.

- **Forest:** The forest style recreates the look of trees growing together in a dense forest setting. The branches intertwine and overlap, creating a canopy of greenery that filters the sunlight. This style often evokes a sense of unity and harmony, as if each tree is connected to the others in a symbiotic relationship.

- **Bunjin**: A style that focuses on creating an illusion of age and maturity through minimalistic design. The tree is often displayed in unconventional containers, adding to its unique charm. The branches are carefully pruned and shaped to resemble the windswept look of a tree that has withstood the test of time. The sparse foliage and exposed roots give the impression of a tree that has weathered many seasons, adding to its sense of wisdom and resilience. The Bunjin style is often associated with contemplation and introspection, as it encourages viewers to reflect on the passage of time and the beauty that can be found in simplicity. This style is particularly popular among bonsai enthusiasts who appreciate the artistry of creating a miniature landscape that tells a story of endurance and grace. Whether displayed in a traditional ceramic pot or an unconventional vessel, a Bunjin bonsai is sure to captivate viewers with its understated elegance and timeless appeal.

- **Broom:** The broom style is characterized by its upright trunk and symmetrical branching pattern, resembling a broom in appearance. This style often represents the tree in motion, with the trunk extending straight into the air. The branches lean back at an oblique angle, creating a sense of momentum that may be compared to a gathering storm. The broom-style bonsai is commonly seen in outdoor gardens or larger display areas, where its grandeur can be fully appreciated. With meticulous pruning and shaping, the broom-style bonsai can become a striking centerpiece, commanding attention with its majestic presence.

These contemporary bonsai styles offer endless possibilities for artistic expression and allow individuals to create truly one-of-a-kind pieces that reflect their taste and vision. Whether you prefer the elegance of the literati style or the dynamic energy of the windswept bonsai, there is a bonsai style perfect for you.

Balance and Harmony in Bonsai Styling

A tree growing in nature uniquely combines individual features that reflect its genetic makeup. It has its own distinct shape, structure, and personality. As the bonsai artist, you want to capture and convey this essence on the bonsai, but how do you do this with limited material? You must use your imagination to recreate a tree's natural beauty through an artistic interpretation of its most characteristic traits. Proper pruning and care can shape the tree into the likeness of a natural tree without compromising its aesthetics. This requires you to pay close attention to the many components of a natural tree and learn how to recreate them effectively on a smaller scale.

The key is achieving balance and harmony between the various elements — the trunk, the branches, the leaves, and other features. The goal is not to make each feature match perfectly (this would look too artificial) but to make all of them work together in harmony (this looks natural). Your bonsai will look like it just came out of the forest when this is achieved.

Before creating a successful bonsai masterwork, you must

first understand what to look for to capture each element of your subject matter. Consider the natural form of a tree: The trunk has branches, which need leaves and twigs to add character and dimension. The branches grow from buds, which are sometimes hidden by leaves or other growth. Leaves are attached to the branches, giving them definition. Then there are the twigs, which develop new buds. These components play an essential role in forming the tree's natural form.

- **The Trunk:** The trunk is the centerpiece of a bonsai and should be its most important feature. The trunk is where all of the character and beauty lies, so it should be the main focus of your design. It can be straight, curved, or twisted. It can have multiple branches or be single-trunked. It can be thick or thin, solid or hollow. All of these characteristics and more are available to you through the use of creativity and imagination. There is no single best type; each trunk has unique traits that must be emphasized and captured in the styling process.

- **The Branches**: Branches are where the leaves live, so they're very important in creating a natural appearance. They add dimension and structure to a tree; they can also create a silhouette to give the bonsai depth and texture. The branches can be straight or curved, depending on the desired aesthetic. Curved branches create a sense of movement and elegance, while straight branches give a more formal and structured look. A bonsai tree should have the branch structure of a natural tree—not too many branches or too few.

- **The Leaves:** Leaves are the most visible components of a tree and make up a large part of its natural form. They add color and texture to the bonsai but also help create depth by breaking up the silhouette, giving your piece a three-dimensional appearance. The leaf's shape can vary; sometimes it's big, and sometimes small. Some leaves are broad, long, and angular, while others are shaped like fans or elaborate patterns. They can be smooth or jagged, pointed or rounded. All of these variations are available to help you create a natural-looking bonsai.

While the trunk, branches, and leaves are the most prominent features of a natural tree, they're not the only ones. A bonsai should reflect its subject matter with all its components—bark, buds, flowers, or fruit—but these are harder to capture on a smaller scale. They require more intricate techniques and are not essential to a successful bonsai, especially for a beginner. However, they can be used to make your design more attractive because they add additional layers of detail and realism.

One technique that can mimic the texture and appearance of natural bark is called jin. Jin involves stripping away bark sections to expose the underlying wood, creating a weathered and aged look. This technique can be applied strategically to certain areas of the bonsai, such as where branches have been pruned or where natural damage would occur over time. Another technique that adds visual interest is called Shari. Shari involves carving grooves or channels into the trunk or branches to simulate natural aging or weathering. This technique can create the illusion of a tree that has been through years of harsh conditions, adding character and depth to your bonsai design. Also, incorporating small buds, flowers, or fruit can bring life and vibrancy to your bonsai. These elements can be created using materials like wire, clay, or preserved plant parts. You can create a true miniature representation of nature by carefully selecting and placing these details throughout your bonsai.

How Bonsai Proportions Are Determined

As you study trees in nature, you'll notice that they have certain proportions carried across the board. These proportions include the ratio of the trunk to branches, the spacing between branches, and the tree's overall height. When designing a bonsai, it is important to replicate these proportions to create a visually appealing and realistic representation.

- **Trunk Size:** The height of a bonsai should be 6–12 times the width of the trunk at its lowest point. This means that a trunk with a width of 3 inches should be 18–36 inches tall, while a tree with a width of 1 inch should be no taller than

6–12 inches tall. These general proportional rules provide a starting point for beginners, but as you gain experience, you will find loopholes to break away from these guidelines to produce more creative yet realistic designs.

- **Branch Placement:** The branches of a bonsai tree should follow a pattern that mimics the growth of a full-sized tree. The lower branches should be longer and thicker, gradually decreasing in size as they move up the trunk. This creates a sense of age and maturity in the bonsai, similar to how a full-sized tree would appear. The spacing between branches should also be proportional. Branches should be evenly spaced along the trunk, with large or heavy branches receiving more space between them than smaller or lighter ones. Studying different tree species and their growth patterns allows you to develop a keen eye for branch placement that adds authenticity to your bonsai design.

- **Foliage Distribution**: Ever-changing weather patterns and the natural pruning process cause trees to produce differently shaped leaves. Not considering these factors when you're growing a bonsai can leave your design looking inauthentic with leaves that are too uniform in shape or position. A bonsai tree's foliage should reflect how a tree would naturally grow, meaning that the proportion of different leaf sizes in your design should reflect the species' typical growth patterns.

- **Trunk Movement:** The movement of the trunk is another important aspect to consider when creating a realistic bonsai design. A straight and rigid trunk may lack character and fail to capture the essence of a mature tree. Instead, incorporating gentle curves and bends in the trunk can give it a sense of age and gracefulness. You can do this using wiring techniques or selecting trees with naturally exciting trunk shapes.

Bonsai's design should follow the natural layout of the tree species and strive to mimic the beauty and complexity of a full-sized tree in miniature form. A bonsai artist can create a captivating and lifelike representation of nature by considering proportions, branch placement, foliage density, and trunk movement. The careful selection of tree species, attention to detail in pruning and shaping techniques, and patience in allowing the bonsai to develop over time are all essential elements in achieving a realistic design.

Chapter Five

Chapter 5: Bonsai Pot Selection and Display

What's the point of spending hours on selective chopping, wiring, and styling a bonsai tree if it's just going to be put in an ugly pot? It may seem like a silly question, but pots are a vital part of any bonsai display. They not only house the roots of your tree; they also create form and tell a visual story that complements the bonsai's silhouette and aura.

Bonsai Pots: The Art of Style and Use

A bonsai tree doesn't simply need a pot but a beautiful and interesting one. Pots are an extension of the art itself and can be just as important as the tree itself. The pot's design should complement and extend the bonsai design, which can make the experience of viewing it even more rewarding. Some common conventions to follow are recreating a style similar to the style that your tree was styled in, having matching colors between pot and tree, or even having complementary colors.

Like the bonsai tree, pots capture the imagination as they tell you a story. They add an extra dimension to the tree and help create a wonderful atmosphere. Without them, your bonsai will stand alone, like a piece of sculpture you placed in your living room, without any interactivity with the room or anything else. The pot is the bridge to creating a cohesive and living display.

What Makes a Good Pot?

You want your tree to stand out in all aspects, not just in styling. To do this, try to get a pot that complements the tree as much as possible without taking away from what makes the tree great in itself. You need to consider many factors when choosing a pot for your bonsai tree. For example:

Size

First of all, you need to consider the size of the tree and the size of the pot. If a pot is too big or too small for a tree, it can look extremely awkward and out of place. The pot should generally be as tall as the trunk's diameter above the surface roots. Sometimes you can go out of that range, but generally speaking, this is a good guideline to follow.

Feminine or Masculine

Is your tree feminine or masculine? A tree is usually a combination of both, so the question will be which sex is dominant. This is the most critical guideline to remember while selecting a pot. Curves, elegance, smooth bark, and thin branches are considered feminine characteristics, while strength, aged bark, deadwood, a robust trunk, and dense branches are male characteristics. The finest containers to use for feminine trees are circular, shallow ones. Rectangular ones are OK with gentle lines, delicate feet, and hollowed-out edges. Masculine trees work well with angular, somewhat deeper pots with strong lines, robust feet, lips on the rim, and bulging edges. However, if you're unsure of which sex is dominant, or you want to be safe, you can use a bonsai pot that is circular or drum-shaped, which is suitable for either sex.

Shape and Form

Remember that a bonsai is an art form, and any good piece of art should present the viewer with beautiful curves. Bonsai trees are designed to sit on display; therefore, the shape and form of the pot you choose should be similar to what would be expected for a showpiece on display. This means that you should go for shapes that are pleasing to the eye, not ones that are awkward or too simple. The shape should also be suitable for the tree, not taking away from what the tree artistically portrays.

Color

The purpose of selecting the most appropriate color is to create harmony with your tree. You can accomplish this by matching the color of the container to any aspect of your tree. You can work with the bark, the color of the leaves, deadwood, flowers, or fruits. Use a neutral hue that mirrors the tree's bark for deciduous trees that change leaf color in the fall. By doing this, the pot color will match beautifully with the tree regardless of the season.

Texture

Consider the sort of tree you have: coniferous or deciduous. For coniferous trees, the majority of bonsai artists prefer unglazed pots. Unglazed pots have a rough and textured surface, perfect for bringing out the ancient look typical of coniferous trees. For deciduous trees, a glazed pot is often preferred to amplify the tree's allure with the change of the seasons. Glazed pots provide a smooth and polished surface that complements the elegance and grace of deciduous trees. The glossy finish adds a touch of sophistication and enhances the visual appeal when the tree undergoes seasonal transformations.

Personal Taste

Sometimes, there is no right or wrong way to do it. When making your final decision, choose a pot that inspires and speaks to you. If you don't feel like it's the right pot for your particular tree, it probably isn't. Trust your instincts and choose a pot that aligns with your personal taste and style. Whether you prefer a minimalist design or something more ornate, there are endless options to choose from. Consider the color, shape, and texture of the pot, as well as any decorative elements that catch your eye. Remember, the pot is not just a vessel for your tree but also an expression of your own creativity and individuality. So, take your time, explore different options, and find the perfect pot that will bring out the beauty of your tree in a way that resonates with you.

Categories of Bonsai Pots

Many different categories of Bonsai Pots offer different styles and aesthetics. The main categories are:

Shape

Circular

This is the most common shape for bonsai pots. Its curved outer rim gently frames the tree, creating a harmonious and balanced composition. The circular shape symbolizes unity and completeness, enhancing the overall aesthetic appeal of the bonsai. It is suitable for a wide range of tree species and styles, from formal upright to cascading. While it can be shallow or deep, the optimal depth is about one-third of the trunk's height.

Rectangular

A rectangular pot offers a more contemporary and structured look to your bonsai. Its clean lines and sharp edges create a sense of stability and strength, making it ideal for masculine or angular tree designs. This shape also provides ample space for root development, allowing the tree to thrive and grow vigorously.

Drum

This pot resembles a large drum and can combine both circular and rectangular shapes into one design. It is built to accommodate large trees with multiple trunks or even small trees planted in groups of three. It is also particularly effective for older trees and cascading designs.

Oval

An oval pot provides a distinct silhouette and creates a more three-dimensional effect. It is similar in appearance to the drum pot but is flatter and wider. This shape works well for larger trees and trees with shorter trunks and low-growing branches. It can also be used for group plantings that create a larger canopy.

Octagon

This relatively new shape is best suited for irregular or asymmetrical plant motifs. The octagonal shape complements and enhances the tree's natural imperfections, resulting in an appealing composition. While it works well for all styles of bonsai trees, it can also be used to create a beautiful landscape display.

Material

Ceramic

Ceramic pots are popular among bonsai enthusiasts due

to their versatility and durability. They come in various colors, textures, and finishes, allowing you to select one that complements your tree's characteristics. Ceramic pots also provide excellent insulation for the roots, protecting them from extreme temperatures.

Wooden

For a more natural and organic feel, wooden pots are another option for bonsai trees. They add a rustic and traditional touch to the overall aesthetic of the tree. Wooden pots are typically made from materials like cedar or pine, known for their durability and resistance to rot. They also provide good insulation for the roots and allow for proper drainage. A drawback, however, is that wooden pots require regular maintenance to prevent decay and ensure longevity.

Stone

Stone pots are a decorative and artistic alternative to ceramic pots. They add a sense of refinement and elegance and are typically made from granite or marble. There are also stone pots polished to exhibit the finest glazes and textures, adding a luxurious touch to any garden or patio. Stone pots are incredibly durable and can withstand harsh weather conditions, making them a long-lasting option for outdoor use. Their weight also provides stability, preventing them from tipping over easily. However, it's best to consider the weight of stone pots when choosing their placement because they can be difficult to move once filled with soil and plants. They also require occasional cleaning to maintain their pristine appearance and prevent moss or algae growth. Overall, stone pots are a timeless choice that combines beauty and durability in the world of gardening.

Appearance

Glazed

Glazed pottery is the most popular type of bonsai pot among enthusiasts. It is ideal for any species and style of tree. Its smooth, shiny finish adds glamor to the tree's natural beauty and complements the overall aesthetic of the bonsai. Glazed pots come in a wide range of colors and patterns, allowing for endless possibilities for creating visually stunning displays. The vibrant hues and intricate designs can enhance the artistic appeal of the bonsai, making it a focal point in any setting. Moreover, the glazed surface protects against weather elements, preventing water absorption and minimizing the risk of cracking or fading over time.

Unglazed

Unglazed pots, also known as unglazed clay or terracotta pots, offer a more traditional and rustic look to bonsai trees. These porous pots allow better air circulation and moisture regulation around the roots. The natural, earthy tones of unglazed pots blend harmoniously with the organic beauty of bonsai trees, creating a sense of harmony between nature and art. Moreover, unglazed pots age gracefully over time, developing a unique patina that adds character and depth to the overall composition.

The Art of Positioning and Display

Bonsai trees are living works of art, so it's important to consider every aspect that makes them unique and special. Consider the following factors when deciding on a specific way to display your bonsai tree:

Location

Bonsai trees offer endless possibilities for how they can be displayed both indoors and out. They can be placed indoors on a windowsill to take advantage of natural light or on a decorative shelf to create a focal point in a room. Or they can be positioned outdoors in a garden bed or on a patio to enhance the general landscape. The location should provide the right balance of sunlight and shade for your specific type of bonsai tree.

Height and Perspective

Consider the height and perspective from which your bonsai tree will be viewed. Placing it at eye level allows for easy appreciation of its intricate details while positioning it at different heights can create visual interest and depth. You can experiment with different angles and viewpoints to find the most visually appealing position for your bonsai tree.

Complementary Elements

Incorporating complementary elements can enhance the display of your tree. Consider adding small accent plants, rocks, or figurines that complement the style and aesthetic of your bonsai. These elements should not overpower the bonsai but rather enhance its natural beauty. For example, placing small rocks or pebbles at the base of a bonsai can create a sense of grounding and stability. Adding a miniature figurine that matches the theme or style of the tree can add a touch of whimsy and personality. These subtle enhancements can add depth and character, ensuring your bonsai tree gets the attention it deserves.

Temperature

Bonsai trees are delicate plants that require a certain temperature range for optimal growth. The ideal temperature depends on the type of bonsai tree, so you should know your tree species' temperature requirements before making any adjustments. Generally, most bonsai trees thrive in temperatures between 60 and 75 degrees Fahrenheit. Still, it is better to do some research and understand the specific needs of your bonsai tree, as some may require cooler or warmer conditions. Maintaining a consistent temperature is key because drastic fluctuations can stress your tree and affect its growth. Consider placing your bonsai in a location that offers protection from extreme heat or cold, like near a window with indirect sunlight or in a controlled environment like a greenhouse. Monitoring the temperature regularly will ensure you provide the ideal conditions for your bonsai's longevity.

Color Harmony

Colors and textures that complement each other create visual interest, but using too many different colors and textures can overwhelm the viewer. Although a handful of general color schemes exist, color combinations are not set in stone. For example, a mixture of blues and greens can create a calming effect, whereas mixing reds and oranges can create a warm atmosphere in stark contrast to the trees' surroundings. The key is to find the right balance of colors that work together naturally without overwhelming your aesthetic sense.

You can explore analogous colors adjacent to each other on the color wheel. Combining different shades of blues and purples or greens and yellows can create a rich, dynamic look. Contrasting colors, on the other hand, can be used to create visual interest in your bonsai tree. Pairing complementary colors like red and green or purple and yellow can create a striking effect that grabs attention and sets the scene.

We have options for virtually every product or service we need in the modern world. The same can be said about bonsai pots. Many different types and styles of pots can be used for bonsai trees, each with its own benefits and drawbacks. The choice of pot to use for your bonsai tree depends on your preferences and needs. But, no matter which type of pot you choose, remember to consider your bonsai tree's unique shape and personality when choosing the one for you. With the proper knowledge and healthy respect for your bonsai tree, the right pot will help you cultivate a long and fruitful relationship with your living art.

Chapter Six

Chapter 6: Bonsai Care and Maintenance

Bonsai trees are intentionally grown to be much smaller than their natural proportions, so they typically require much attention and care to maintain their form and remain healthy. Each Bonsai has its own unique shape, size, and personality, which is so much fun to take care of. However, there are a few things that you should be aware of before committing yourself to this type of lifelong hobby.

Seasonal Care for Bonsai Trees

Working on a tree only when the best results can be obtained while interfering as little as possible with nature's activities makes sense. Every intervention needs a clear goal, and stressing a plant will only hinder its development rather than speed it up, so timing your work is critical.

Plants go through several stages in a single year:

1. Winter hibernation

2. Spring growth

3. Summer dormancy

4. Autumn decline and renewal

Each of these four seasons brings different health and stress levels to trees based on location, weather conditions, and temperature variations. Seasonal care for bonsai trees is critical for maintaining their health and beauty throughout the year. During winter hibernation, bonsai trees enter a period of dormancy where their growth slows down significantly. As spring arrives, they begin their growth phase and emerge into a whole new season of life and energy. Summer brings dormancy again, but not in the same passive state as winter. Instead, the trees are now ready to enjoy summer's warmer temperatures and higher humidity. As autumn approaches, the trees undergo a natural decline and renewal process. Leaves may change color and eventually fall off, signaling the transition into dormancy once more.

The proper timing of your seasonal care practices is what stands between you and the bonsai masterpiece you've always dreamed of. Remember the four stages of a plant's year and care for your Bonsai accordingly.

Winter Hibernation

The absence of leaves prevents photosynthesis and any activity in the organs. The above-ground portion of the tree requires neither light nor fertilizer. The roots, however, remain active and continue to draw nutrients from the soil, so water must be kept in adequate supply throughout this period, as it can be detrimental to the tree if its roots are dry for too long. There is no need for fertilizer during the winter because little growth occurs. In fact, fertilizer use during this time can be harmful, but if you choose to fertilize during the winter, apply it early in the season. Most Bonsai can be repotted over the winter, but the safest time to do this is in the weeks leading up to the early spring rebirth when there is no longer a risk of strong cold damaging the roots. If you want to repot a tree in the dead of winter, ensure it's in a frost-free location, but not in a very warm room, because you don't want to risk any untimely growth.

Late winter is also an excellent season for structural, replacement, and maintenance pruning. Structural pruning is the removal of parts of the Bonsai that are not considered essential to its overall form. During this time, you can remove things like main branches and excess trunk diameter. Replacement pruning involves reducing the height or length of a bonsai's branches to make the Bonsai's form more compact or refined. Maintenance pruning is similar to replacement pruning, but it is performed only on already trained branches whose length needs to be reduced.

You can also begin training the main branch or trunk for the upcoming growing season in late winter by wiring it in place.

Spring Growth

After a long winter of rest, trees are eager for action. This is when new leaves come out to help speed up photosynthesis and the rejuvenating process for the tree, hopefully increasing its chances of making it through another growing season and giving it the boost of energy needed for growth. This is an important stage in the tree's year as it sets the course for future growth and determines how the above-ground portion of your Bonsai will look. Watering and fertilizing need to be done regularly during this period so that the tree does not become dehydrated or receive excess nutrients. You can repot trees in mid-spring, but keep in mind that they will grow more rapidly than in other seasons and that putting them in larger containers means they will have to transition even more quickly from old growth to new growth. It will be another active growth period for the above-ground portion of many trees. For most deciduous trees, this is when they have their most significant amount of vitality.

Summer Dormancy

The Bonsai is now dormant, experiencing a period where no leaves develop. The roots breathe a sigh of relief. Water and fertilizer are still required for the tree to remain healthy. Still, it is also a good time for pruning so that any excess growth can be trimmed from branches by reducing the length or width of the branches to refine or focus the Bonsai's shape and to allow for future growth. This period gives deciduous species their shape and is an ideal time for working on the branches of the tree while they are still relaxed and compliant to manipulation. Pruning during this period helps maintain the Bonsai's aesthetic appeal and promotes better airflow and sunlight penetration, which are crucial for the tree's health. Pruning should be approached carefully, ensuring each cut is made at the right angle and distance from the branch collar to prevent unnecessary damage or disease. Removing dead or diseased branches during this time helps prevent infection and encourages new growth. As you carefully shape and refine your Bonsai branches, take a few moments to step back and assess them. Imagine how their shape and size will develop over the coming year, and use this to guide your pruning decisions. With a bit of patience, the tree will follow the path you create and develop into the mature form you envisioned.

Autumn Decline and Renewal

The tree is now beginning its annual decline, which signals the season of renewal. This stage provides new challenges for the bonsai artist: leaves are falling off trees, branches are becoming less pliable, and an increase in nutrients is required to nourish the roots as growth slows down. The bonsai tree is now gradually preparing itself for the long winter ahead. This is an ideal time to remove any unwanted growth and to repot a tree if it has been growing in the same container for several years. During the autumn decline, you can trim back the above-ground portion of your Bonsai, especially the foliage, to prepare it for the increasing cold that comes with winter. This is also a good time to check on any pruning you did in the summer and ensure you have not accidentally cut too close to the branch collar or other important areas of your Bonsai.

Bonsai care methods change with each season, and while they are not always drastic adjustments, even small changes can result in significant differences in the tree. The key to success is to focus on each Bonsai individually, identifying its current needs and anticipating future needs. Even the smallest adjustment to your Bonsai's care can make or break its chances of thriving.

Pest and Disease Control

Disease is the leading cause of death for bonsai trees. Most diseases are caused by poor sanitation or improper care. The first step in preventing disease is good sanitation. Keeping your tools clean and using high-quality soil and healthy stock will go a long way toward preventing and controlling disease in your trees. Another thing is regularly inspecting your Bonsai for any signs of disease or pests. Your tree should not be ignored if you notice any unusual spots, discoloration, or wilting leaves. Perform a full inspection of the tree immediately to assess its general health. Next, examine the rest of your Bonsai container to ensure it is clean and free of any pests or unusual activity. Many pest and disease control methods exist, including organic options like neem oil or insecticidal soap. If you decide to go the chemical route, carefully follow the instructions and dosage recommendations to avoid harming your tree. Proper watering techniques, adequate sunlight, and air circulation can also help strengthen your Bonsai's immune system and reduce disease risk. With good care and disease prevention, a healthy bonsai will venture into the bitter winter without fear.

How to Water Your Bonsai Tree

Watering your Bonsai means striking a balance between underwatering and overwatering. Underwatering a bonsai tree will not kill it, but it will prevent it from absorbing the nutrients in the soil that it needs to grow. Overwatering can cause root rot and possibly kill your tree by creating a situation where the roots cannot breathe.

Before watering your Bonsai, check the soil for moisture. If you are using a humidity tray for an indoor, tropical, or semi-tropical Bonsai, water is not needed as frequently as for an outdoor, temperate one. However, check the soil's moisture level daily to ensure that your Bonsai isn't left in an uncomfortable situation. You may have to water your Bonsai up to three times a week or even more, depending on the condition of the soil and the weather. It is helpful to look at your Bonsai's general health when determining whether or not it needs water. Highly stressed plants need more water than healthy ones, but if you are unsure when your Bonsai needs water, err on the side of caution and use a moisture meter.

When you've decided that the soil is a little dry and the tree needs watering, use a watering can with a fine nozzle to fully soak the entire root system. Continue watering until water drains out of the holes underneath the pot. This way, you're sure the water is going where needed. If you keep an indoor Bonsai, place it in your kitchen sink and properly water it before keeping it in its initial position. The best water for bonsai watering is rainwater because it is completely chemical-free, but regular tap water will do if you do not have access to it.

Repotting

Repotting is a necessary part of bonsai care. It is an opportunity to evaluate your tree's health, organize its branches and main trunk, and redirect or trim any damaged or unhealthy growth. Many bonsai artists say that repotting should only be performed every 3–5 years on most trees, though there are exceptions to this rule. In a healthy bonsai tree, the roots grow so they can be easily removed from the pot. The idea is never to repot your tree when its roots are compacted and tangled. Trimming small sections of the roots will help keep them loose and ready for extraction if you need to wait a little extra time before repotting the tree.

Choosing the right time of year for repotting will also save your tree from undue stress. Spring is usually considered the ideal time for repotting bonsai trees, though this can vary depending on your climate. Spring is a time of renewal and rebirth; trees prepare themselves for the rapid growth that comes with summer and are naturally active, so you can repot in early spring before new growth begins. This will allow the tree to recover quickly and establish itself in its new pot. You can also repot in late winter, during the transition between dormancy and spring reawakening, although you risk losing the delicate roots to frost.

When repotting, using a well-draining soil mix specifically designed for bonsai trees is best. This ensures that excess water can quickly drain away, preventing root rot and other issues. After repotting, regular watering, fertilizing, and pruning are necessary to keep the tree thriving. Remember to monitor the tree's health closely and make adjustments as needed. With patience and dedication, your bonsai tree will continue to flourish for years without complications from unhealthy root growth or neglectful repotting practices.

The Perfect Bonsai Soil

The right soil will give your bonsai tree the nutrients it needs to grow while allowing excess water to drain. It should also offer proper aeration and water retention. There are hundreds of different types of potting soils on the market today, but not all are well-suited for every bonsai tree. Many commercial brands provide ready-mixed soils, but doing it yourself saves money and gives you more control over the exact combination for your specific tree species.

Inorganic soil is particle-based, meaning you can see small bits of stone and sand in the soil. This soil type allows water to drain quickly and oxygen to reach the roots. Organic soil, on the other hand, contains no particle-based material. It is made from organic matter like compost and peat moss. This kind of soil is not as structured, so it is not well-suited for Bonsai. It holds water and nutrients better than inorganic soil, which is usually good for other plants, but it isn't aerated enough for Bonsai, so the roots cannot breathe and will slowly die from suffocation. It also tends to retain more water than is required for Bonsai, which will eventually cause your tree to drown.

Both inorganic and organic soils can be mixed to create the perfect mix for your bonsai needs. Ideal soil mixes for Bonsai usually contain compost, pumice, akadama, and lava rock. Akadama is a kind of Japanese clay that has been hard-baked. It is made particularly for Bonsai and is sold at most bonsai stores. If you intend to add akadama to your soil mix, know that it must be sifted before it is added to the mix and that it begins to break down after approximately two years, reducing aeration. This means trees with akadama should be repotted every two years or risk suffocation.

Pumice and lava rocks are both excellent for drainage.

They contribute to the water drainage in your soil as well as the soil's overall structure and ability to hold nutrients. Compost is a well-decomposed organic material. It adds nutrients and humus to the soil, but compost can easily become too wet and compacted when used by itself. To add more structure to your soil mix, you will need to combine it with other inorganic particle-based materials. The particle-based materials will allow the compost to breathe and prevent it from becoming too wet.

Bonsai is a very rewarding hobby. You can grow, take care of, and watch your bonsai tree blossom into a beautiful miniature version of what it once was. It will bring you great pleasure to watch your carefully nurtured tree grow and change as you take care of it over the years, but you MUST take care of it for it to grow. A good bonsai tree should never look like it's suffering, and it will show if you are not providing it with the proper care.

Chapter Seven

Chapter 7: Advanced Bonsai Techniques

At some point in your bonsai journey, you'll realize that providing bonsai care may not be enough to create the tree of your dreams. This is when more advanced techniques come in handy, and that's what this chapter is about - how to create the most visually appealing trees with professional-grade techniques—from air-layering (a technique focusing on balancing new growth) to approach grafting (a masterful process for creating complex shapes) and thread grafting (a method that allows you to manipulate the direction of growth). These advanced techniques require a deep understanding of the tree's physiology and a delicate touch, but the results are truly remarkable. Air-layering, for example, allows you to create new roots on a branch while it is still attached to the tree, resulting in a stronger and more visually pleasing structure. On the other hand, approach grafting enables you to merge two separate trees into one, creating unique and intricate designs. Thread grafting takes precision and patience, as it involves carefully threading a branch through a small hole in another branch to redirect its growth. By incorporating these advanced techniques into your bonsai practice, you can elevate your creations to new heights and achieve the artistic vision you've always wanted.

Air-Layering

Air-layering, also called Toriki in Japanese, is a slightly more complex method of propagating Bonsai. It is the process of forcing a tree or branch to grow new roots at a specific spot by blocking the flow of nutrients from the current root system. This technique can reduce the length of a trunk, produce better surface roots, or make a branch grow as a distinct tree. The best time to air-layer is in the spring when the tree has already begun to grow after its winter hibernation. The main goals of air-layering are to create a new root system that is stronger and more aesthetically pleasing than the original one, as well as a stronger root system that can help the tree recover from damage.

How to:

There are two ways you can air-layer your bonsai tree:

1. **Tourniquet Technique**: To partially stop the flow of nutrients, the tourniquet technique involves tightly encircling the trunk or branch with copper wire. The stream of nutrients will be reduced when the trunk or branch thickens, pushing it to develop new roots immediately above the

wire. This technique is used for trees that develop slowly and require more time to establish new roots since they won't survive the more aggressive ring approach. Tree species, including junipers, azaleas, maples, elms, and pines, are suited for the tourniquet technique.

2. **Ring Technique**: The ring technique involves removing a ring of bark from the area of the trunk or branch where new roots should sprout. Roots must form right away for the area above the ring to survive. The ring must be large enough to keep the tree from healing and closing the opening but not so large as to restrict the tree's growth. This aggressive process usually works on species like ligusters, willows, and beeches.

Success Rate: The success rate of air-layering can be greatly increased by following a few simple rules:

1. The tree must be healthy and developed. Young, new trees that have yet to bloom will not survive the process.

2. The tree's root system must be strong. It is best to have at least two healthy roots (or three if the tree has been injured before growing) for the root system to survive.

3. The area with new roots must be protected from rain or excessive direct sunlight. The fresh roots

may rot if exposed to excessive moisture or direct sunlight.

4. Keep it simple. The more complicated you get with air-layering, the longer it takes for your tree to recover and the higher the risk of failure.

5. Air-layer in the spring or early summer because some tree species need more time to heal after having their bark removed.

Performing the Tourniquet Technique

1. At the spot where you would like new roots to grow, wrap a piece of copper wire around the trunk or branch.

2. The wire should be thick enough to cut halfway through the bark of the branch or trunk.

3. Apply a bit of rooting hormone to the cut and then cover it with plastic wrap filled with sufficient sphagnum moss. Soon enough, you will have your new root system.

Performing the Ring Technique

1. Cut two parallel incisions around the branch's perimeter using a sharp knife. Maintain at least twice the diameter of the branch between the two slots.

2. Remove the bark ring between these two cuts all the way down to the shiny cambium layer.

3. The ring should be broad enough to prevent the tree from bridging the incision. You should also ensure the bark has been completely removed because a tree won't begin to produce new roots unless it feels like it has no other option.

4. Apply rooting hormone and wrap a substantial amount of sphagnum moss over the opening before completely covering it with plastic.

Grafting in Bonsai

Grafting is the process of using a scion (a small shoot of a tree, usually with an established root system) to create a new branch or trunk on a host tree. The scion is cut to fit the desired shape and size of the Bonsai, then attached to the host tree by wrapping it in grafting tape. Grafting allows you to create elaborate and extreme branches that cannot be achieved through styling alone. It can be done using various techniques, such as approach, thread, or scion grafting. Each technique requires precision and careful handling to successfully integrate the scion and rootstock.

The choice of tree species for grafting in Bonsai depends on factors like compatibility, growth habits, and desired aesthetic outcomes. Compatible trees should be chosen with careful observation of the graft's root system and the scion's size and shape. Species that produce strong flowering branches or fast-growing annuals are ideal for grafting. Deciduous trees with thick bark offer a wider range of branching styles, although these can sometimes be more vulnerable to winter damage. Avoid trees that have developed bad habits, like hollow or dead wood, or have very shallow roots because grafting only works on trees with rooted shoots and can grow new roots. The tree should also be healthy because grafting weakens the root system, so it is best to choose younger trees. Trees in poor health often do not survive the transplanting process and end up dying after a few years. By skillfully combining different varieties through grafting techniques, the bonsai artist can create stunning trees that exhibit a harmonious blend of characteristics from multiple species.

How to:

There are three ways to graft in Bonsai:

1. **Approach grafting** is the process of connecting a donor plant with its roots still attached to a recipient plant to change the leaf type of the tree or add branches in desired areas. Approach grafting demands the use of a completely intact donor plant (also known as a 'whip') and connecting it, roots and all, to the receiving plant rather than removing a shoot from the donor plant and putting it into the receiving plant.

2. **Thread grafting** is another method used in

Bonsai grafting. This technique involves threading a small branch or shoot from the donor plant through a hole made in the receiving plant's trunk or branch. The two plants are then secured together, allowing nutrients and water to flow between them. Thread grafting is often used to add new branches or change the direction of growth in a Bonsai tree.

3. **Scion grafting** is a common technique in Bonsai grafting. It involves cutting a small branch or shoot, known as the scion, from the donor plant and attaching it to the receiving plant. The scion is carefully matched to the receiving plant's trunk or branch, ensuring a proper fit. Once attached, the scion and receiving plant are secured together using grafting tape or other materials. This method allows for precise control over the growth and development of the Bonsai tree, as specific traits from the scion can be incorporated into the receiving plant.

Success Rate: Although grafting is a relatively simple process, it still requires much skill and practice. In the end, the success rate depends on whether or not the scion is well-matched to its recipient plant. Sometimes even perfectly matched plants may not survive the transplanting process, so don't be discouraged if you don't get it right the first time. With time and practice, you will be able to develop a knack for matching plants based on a sense of intuition and visual observations.

Advantages

1. Grafting is a highly effective strategy for creating complex branching structures that cannot be achieved through other means.

2. Grafted trees are also more resilient to diseases and pests.

3. Grafting helps improve the variety of a tree's leaves, which can create a more interesting aesthetic appeal.

4. Grafting is also a great way to help a struggling tree survive and thrive in your bonsai collection.

5. Successfully grafting Bonsai trees can be very rewarding and fun!

Disadvantages

1. Grafting trees is a time-consuming process that requires much practice to master.

2. Not all trees can be successfully grafted, so it's important to research and consider your options before attempting this technique.

3. Even if the grafting is successful, the tree may still die anyway due to transplant shock at a later date.

Performing Approach Grafting

1. Select a healthy scion and receiving plant for grafting. Your chances of success increase if you choose compatible plants with similar growth habits.

2. Prepare the scion by making a diagonal cut at the base, ensuring it is clean and free from diseases or pests.

3. Similarly, prepare the receiving plant by making a corresponding diagonal cut on the trunk or branch where the scion will be attached.

4. Align the cambium layers of the scion and receiving plant, where the graft union will form.

5. Carefully place the scion onto the receiving plant, ensuring a snug fit between the two surfaces.

6. Securely wrap the graft union with grafting tape or other materials to hold it in place and provide support during healing.

7. Monitor the grafted tree closely for signs of successful union, such as new growth emerging from the scion.

8. Continue caring for the grafted tree by properly watering, fertilizing, and protecting it from pests and diseases. Regularly check the graft to ensure

it remains secure and free from any signs of infection or failure. You must be patient during the healing process, as the graft may take several weeks or even months to integrate and establish itself fully. With proper care and attention, the grafted tree should eventually thrive and grow into a healthy and productive plant.

Performing Thread Grafting

1. The branch used for the threading should be allowed to grow long and strong enough to provide a sturdy base for the graft.

2. Before drilling the hole in the trunk into which the thread graft will be placed, examine the size of the drill bit in relation to the size of the thread graft branch. The bit should be no wider than the biggest buds that will be placed through the graft.

3. Now drill into the trunk from one side and exit through the other at the spot where the thread graft will be inserted. Check to make sure the hole is clean and straight.

4. If you're working with deciduous material, the thread graft must first be wired into place using aluminum wire. Bend the thread-grafted branch carefully back around to the place where it will be put into the trunk. Firmly hold the thread-graft-

ed branch and put it carefully into the trunk through the hole you previously made.

5. Leave the tree alone for the rest of the growing season, allowing the thread graft to develop and grow. Remove the cut paste the next spring and examine the graft. If it is still secure, you can remove the original branch and allow the new branch to grow naturally.

Performing Scion Grafting

1. Select a healthy scion branch or shoot that is long enough to be properly grafted onto the desired tree.

2. Shortly after detaching the scion from the donor plant, make two incisions at its base using a sharp, sterile grafting knife. The first incision will be longer than the second and progressively slanted. It is made by holding the scion in one hand, pressing the knife against it, and slowly bringing the scion towards yourself while softly pushing the knife away. Make a somewhat shorter, sharper-angled incision on the other side of the scion. This second cut will be around half to two-thirds the length of the first.

3. Now, Wrap some grafting tape around the scion from the base of the leaves, ensuring it is snug and

secure. Pulling the tape too firmly may crush the leaves, so don't do that, but make sure it is tight enough to prevent water from leaking in or out.

4. Next, decide where the scion will be grafted onto the receiving plant and make a precise incision using a grafting knife. The incision should be long enough to accommodate the whole length of the previously cut scion and deep enough to reach the heartwood.

5. Now, carefully slide the cut end of the scion into the flap on the recipient tree. The longer cut on the scion should rest against the trunk, while the shorter cut faces outward. Align the donor scion's cambium layer with the cambium layer of the receiving plant as you insert the scion.

6. Finally, secure the graft with more grafting tape, ensuring it is firm enough to hold the scion in place but not so tight as to crush the leaves or cut into the wood of the scion. There must be no room for moisture to seep in because the scion graft will probably fail if water gets past the tape and causes rot.

Grafting Bonsai is an art and a science, so don't take your graft failure personally. If your graft fails, use the scion from a different tree and try again. If you're still unsuccessful, select a different grafting method for your next try. Patience is the key to success when grafting Bonsai, so settle in for the long haul and keep trying until it sticks.

Chapter Eight

Chapter 8: Bonsai Exhibition and Future Journey

A bonsai exhibition is a captivating display of meticulously cultivated miniature trees, showcasing the artistry and skill of bonsai enthusiasts. It is a platform where bonsai artists worldwide come together to exhibit their finest creations, each tree telling a unique story. A bonsai exhibition aims to appreciate and celebrate the beauty, harmony, and tranquility that these living works of art bring to our lives. It is an opportunity for both novices and experts to learn from one another and be inspired by the incredible diversity of bonsai styles and techniques on display. Meticulous attention to detail is required to prepare your Bonsai for such an exhibition. From selecting the perfect tree to diligently pruning, wiring, and styling it with precision, every step contributes to creating a masterpiece that will captivate viewers.

Preparing Your Bonsai for Exhibition

Once you have chosen the perfect bonsai tree for the exhibition, you must properly prepare it to ensure it looks its best on the big day. This involves several key steps that will help showcase the tree's beauty and create a visually stunning display.

Pruning and Styling

The first step in preparing your bonsai tree for showcasing is to properly prune and style it a few months before the big day. As you know, a bonsai artist must first study the natural form of a tree and reshape it into its ideal shape using wire, pruning, or both. Branches should be placed where they appear most natural and create harmony with other branches on the tree. This process may sound complicated, with seemingly endless possibilities of where to put branches and wire, but it is actually a process of elimination. The best results come from placing branches and wire in the most visually pleasing positions, so keep in mind that while a tree is ultimately an artistic expression of nature, there is a bit of wiggle room to create a more minimalistic and streamlined appearance.

Some trees may require more pruning than others, depending on their size. If the tree has grown too tall and will not fit inside the transport case, it must be pruned before being transported to the exhibition space. Proper pruning before exhibiting your bonsai tree will also prevent branches from becoming damaged during transport.

It will help to display the tree's shape and form to its full potential.

Choosing a Display Stand

Each bonsai showcase must include a stand. It is critical to pick the precise stand to be used with each specimen a month or two before the show, to ensure that the chosen stand will be ready in time. A stand serves as a frame for your work of art. It should complement your Bonsai rather than detract from it. You've chosen the wrong option if somebody says, "What a beautiful stand" instead of "What a beautiful bonsai." Stands range from complex and expensive to simple and affordable. The best display stand will showcase the contrast between the tree and its environment.

Size, form, style, texture, color, and finish in relation to the Bonsai and container are all crucial factors to consider when choosing a stand. As a beginner, it will help to sift through different bonsai magazines and exhibition websites. See how bonsai are placed on stands and try to figure out what is good or bad about the presentation. This will give you a sense of how a stand might be used, how it is built, and the right interaction between your Bonsai, container, and stand.

Using Accent Pieces

The proper accent display pieces can add elegance to your Bonsai. Accent pieces are ornamental and decorative elements placed on top of or below the base of a bonsai tree to be displayed. Accent pieces can range from simple ornaments such as wire and bamboo poles to intricately sculpted wood artworks.

Decorated background panels, thick stone imitation and concrete, stone mosaics, and metal artwork coated in plaster can all add interest to your bonsai display. Accent pieces are decorative but not the main focus of attention. Remember that you are creating a showcase for a tree, not the accent piece. A single piece of wood decorated with carvings will work better as an accent piece than a massive sculpture that might look like it has been dropped in the middle of the Bonsai.

Moss and Soil Dressing

Next, you'll need to dress up your Bonsais soil to give it a professional touch. One way to do this is by adding a layer of moss on top of the soil. Moss adds visual appeal and helps retain moisture in the soil, creating a more suitable environment for your Bonsai roots. Moss can be easily obtained from your local garden center, or you can even collect it from your backyard. Another option for dressing up the soil is to use decorative rocks or pebbles, which can add texture and enhance the aesthetic of your bonsai display.

Decorative rocks or pebbles can be strategically placed around the base of the bonsai tree to create a natural and harmonious look. These rocks can also serve a practical purpose by acting as a barrier to prevent soil erosion and keep the tree stable in its pot. When choosing rocks or pebbles, it helps to consider the size, color, and texture that will complement the overall design of your Bonsai. You can opt for smooth river rocks for a serene and polished look or rough and jagged rocks for a more rugged and organic feel. You can even mix different types of rocks to create a visually interesting and dynamic composition. Experimenting with different rock sizes and shapes can add depth and dimension to your bonsai display. Remember to arrange the rocks to mimic natural formations, like a river bank or shoreline.

You can add an accent color to the soil using a dark container. Plant your Bonsai in a black or dark-colored container to make it stand out from the background. This will enhance the aesthetic appeal of your bonsai tree and create a more realistic and captivating landscape.

Judgment Criteria for Bonsai Exhibitions

Criteria and standards for judging bonsai exhibitions can vary depending on the specific event or organization. However, some common factors that are often considered are the general health and vitality of the bonsai tree, the skill and technique demonstrated in its styling and pruning, the balance and proportion of its branches and foliage, and the overall artistic presentation of the display. Judges may also consider factors such as the age and rarity of the tree species and any unique or innovative design elements incorporated into the composition.

Some judges may also consider the level of difficulty in

maintaining the bonsai tree and the level of mastery displayed by the artist in creating the composition. The impact and emotional response elicited by the display can also play a significant role in the judging process. The health and condition of the tree's root system might also be factored into the decision, as might the artistic use of the pot and background. Judges might also take note of the quality and variety of accent display pieces used to enhance the composition.

In some situations, judges may consider the history and story behind the bonsai tree, as it adds depth and meaning to the artwork. This can include information about the tree's origin, how it was acquired, or any significant events that have shaped its journey. Understanding the context of the Bonsai can provide valuable insight into the artist's intentions and creative vision and influence the level of appreciation for the work.

Bonsai exhibitions provide the perfect opportunity for beginners to learn more about the art form. You may be inspired by a piece or technique you have never seen before and want to explore further. The best way to keep the learning wheels turning is by constantly exposing yourself to demonstrations, workshops, videos, and other forms of bonsai education. Experiment with different styles, techniques, and compositions and seek feedback from others in the community to develop your unique style.

Bonsai communities are often places of creativity and innovation. Turning to other bonsai artists for support, inspiration, and guidance can be beneficial when working on your Bonsai. You can also seek mentorship from a more experienced artist to learn how to refine your skills as an aspiring bonsai artist. Thankfully, the Internet is full of resources like blogs, forums, and online tutorials that can help you learn the nuances of bonsai cultivation and create stunning compositions that truly inspire you.

Conclusion

The art of Bonsai is a captivating journey that intertwines nature, creativity, and patience. It is not just about shaping trees but about cultivating a deep connection with the natural world and finding joy in its miniature representation. Through this ancient practice, we learn to appreciate the beauty of simplicity and the power of nurturing life in its most delicate form. Bonsai teaches us the value of mindfulness and the importance of being present in the moment as we carefully tend to each branch and leaf. It is a timeless art form that invites us to slow down, reflect, and find stillness during our busy lives.

Bonsai also encourages us to develop patience and resilience, as it takes years of dedicated care to shape and train the miniature tree into its desired form. This art serves as a reminder that growth and transformation are gradual processes that require commitment and perseverance. By immersing ourselves in the art of Bonsai, we can find solace and a sense of harmony with nature, yet the practice is not simply about trees; it is an endeavor to find balance and harmony in our lives. Whether we start with a young sapling and watch it grow over the years or begin with a mature bonsai and practice the art of rejuvenation, Bonsai teaches us that every experience is worthy of appreciation and that each moment deserves to be cherished.

References

Allton, C. (2021, September 3). Ultimate Bonsai Manual: All Aspects of Creating Your Own Miniature Gardens: Building Miniature Bonsai Gardens.

Chan, P. (1987, August 1). Bonsai: The Art of Growing and Keeping Miniature Trees. https://doi.org/10.1604/9780890099469

Cordell, S. (2011, June 19). Bonsai Gardening Secrets: A Gardening Guide for Bonsai Beginners with All the Essential Gardening Tips You Need to Know for Growing, Trimming, Sculpting, and Pruning Perfectly Beautiful Bonsai Trees for Your Home.

Lesniewicz, P. (1984, July 1). Bonsai: The Complete Guide to Art and Technique.

MacQuire, L. (2015, October 12). Bonsai Tree Care: A Practical Beginners Guide to Bonsai Gardening.

McRay, M. (2011, March 22). Master the Art of Bonsai Trees.

Mohler, T. (2021, March 5). The Art of Bonsai: Bonsai

Tutorials for Beginners: Beginners Guide about Bonsai.

Pike, D. (1990, October 1). Bonsai: Step by Step to Growing Success. https://doi.org/10.1604/9781852231286

Samson, I., & Samson, R. (1988, October 1). The Creative Art of Bonsai.

Yoshimura, Y., & Halford, G. M. (1997, December 22). The Art of Bonsai: Creation, Care and Enjoyment. https://doi.org/10.1604/9780804820912

Printed in Great Britain
by Amazon